VIEWS·FROM·THE·HOLLYWOOD·HILLS

VIEWS ☆ FROM ☆ THE ☆ HOLLYWOOD ☆ HILLS

PHOTOGRAPHED BY CAREY MORE ☆ WRITTEN BY JULIAN MORE

HENRY
HOLT

First published in the United States in 1987 by
Henry Holt and Company, Inc., 521 Fifth Avenue,
New York, New York 10175

Originally published in Great Britain

LC: 86-18335

ISBN: 0-8050-0206-5

First American Edition
Designed by Bernard Higton
Produced by Pavilion Books Ltd, London
Printed and bound in Spain by Graficas Estella

1   3   5   7   9   10   8   6   4   2

ISBN: 0-8050-0206-5

CONTENTS

Introduction 7
Carey More and Julian More

DREAMS
18

REALITY
56

DREAMS A REALITY
98

Acknowledgments
143

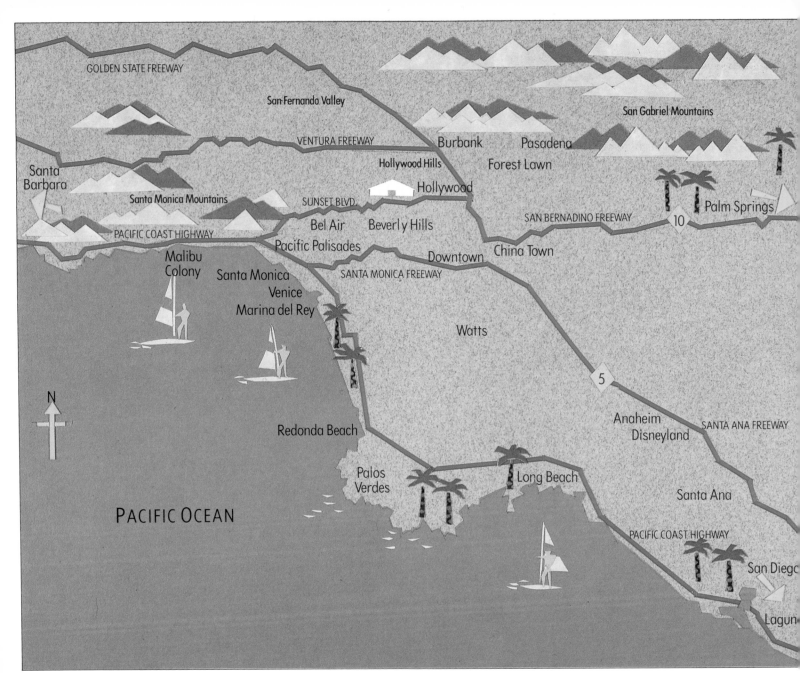

INTRODUCTION

As a child living in London, the mere mention of the States always filled me with awe and mystery — my imagination ran wild. It was not surprising that one day I found myself on a plane bound for America.

What was it really like? In 1978 I found out. I took a plane to New York alone, knowing no one. Woody Allen at Elaine's, whiskey sours, jazz on the borders of Harlem, Sunday brunch, Studio 54, and limos with telephones. The taste was exhilarating — I knew I would be back.

Next stop – Los Angeles, no longer just a name on a departures board. By 1980 I was there and this time the visit became permanent. LA fitted in with my way of thinking. I had endlessly been trying to remove myself from the modelling scene in Europe, and suddenly I saw the freedom expressed in the LA life style. No one knew me, my past was left in Europe. I would make a new start — this time as a photographer.

Most LA residents seem to come from other parts of the world — there to make a new life, build a dream, make a million. Sunny LA presents a very seductive front. But it doesn't come easily.

I struggled for the first two years to make ends meet — taking head shots of waiters dreaming of fame, brochure shots for health spa resorts in Palm Springs and occasional wedding photographs. A faulty flash hired for a marriage sponsored by Elton John at the Bel Air Hotel did not make me too popular with the newlyweds and so ended my short career in weddings.

But luck was mostly on my side, and I found myself house-sitting a beautiful Spanish hacienda just off La Brea, complete with swimming pool, jacuzzi, barbecue and fountained courtyard. Those days were some of the craziest. Endless streams of gay waiters would flock to the pool to bronze their muscled bodies. Parties at the house would go on all night. Jackson Browne and his band had a jam session, and the whole of LA's in-scene came to dance and applaud. The era was unforgettable — I'm surprised 'Hellhouse' (our nickname) did not get into the *National Enquirer*; there were enough scandals and intrigue for an entire issue.

But with its craziness and irresponsibility also came a real sense of meaning and a goal in life. LA provided the foundation for my development as a photographer. My father and I had already started work on our first book *Views from a French Farmhouse*, but I knew that Los Angeles would have to be captured too; it held too many memories to be ignored.

Its beauty is not obvious. The magic of LA lies

between the lines. Driving along yet another grey road, telegraph poles and McDonald signs lulling one into visual torpor, one suddenly awakens to the sight of a sensational Art Deco masterpiece looming out of the architectural wasteland. The incongruity of LA's buildings, people and life styles is a constant surprise, and this is what I have tried to capture.

I will always respect what I learned from the sometimes tough experience of living in LA. You *can* build your dreams there – if you can cut through the bullshit, superficiality, Beautiful People, and endless droning discussions of work, interviews, expectations and disappointments. . .

I have to laugh when I think back to the terrible red roses that landed every day on my doorstep from an amorous real estate tycoon: 'Which will it be – the Porsche, Rolls or MG? Honey, the choice is yours!' Or the pressing encouragement to go on a blind date with 'a really sexy plastic surgeon'. Or perhaps I'd prefer the surf coach.

Well, those were the days. I have chosen *Views from the Hollywood Hills* as my second book in an attempt to share with others my impression of LA's diversity. This time with affection – but also a slightly jaundiced lens.

CAREY MORE, Paris 1985

DOWNTOWN FROM GRIFFITH PARK OBSERVATORY

'I was staying that Christmas in a house on North Selma Drive in the West Hollywood district. The house was Streamline Moderne in style, early thirties, approached by a steep, dead-end driveway. A squirrel scuttled up a palm tree and a blue jay flew out of a eucalyptus. Outside the garage, a handsome young guy had slimy mud all over his hands. A blonde with a figure made for tennis and an English accent was telling him to go call a plumber. Her voice sounded like a plum whose stone had just been extracted by painful dental equipment. I gathered from the Mayfair dialogue they had trouble with the drains. After yesterday's cloud-burst, their slope had begun its usual slipping and sliding. Christmas in LA had begun.'

With apologies to Raymond Chandler.

The small hillside home of my daughter Camilla and her husband Nick owes more to Chandler's private dick, Philip Marlowe, than Frank Lloyd Wright. From this charming but slightly crumbling retro perch on the slopes of the Hollywood Hills, their sundeck takes in the giant posters of Sunset Strip, snow-capped mountains silhouetting Downtown towers, the mock-French turrets of the Chateau Marmont Hotel, neon lights against a rosy-fingered dawn.

The giant posters proclaim the arrival of yet another Christmas kiddie-pic about Outer Space, reminding us that we are nearer to President Reagan's 'Star Wars' than Gloria Swanson's 'Sunset Boulevard'.

The view is a dreamscape, dotted with reminders of reality. Grotesque, surreal images amid the sprawling, unrestrained mass called Slurb. Nearly one hundred miles of it, north to south.

My opening paragraph may be fiction, but the family drainage problem was one of those reminders of reality. When my wife Sheila and I arrived at LAX from Paris, the space-age terminal built for the 1984 Olympics had flooding problems. After immigration formalities in its dry top section, rather than let us swim for our bags in the Olympic pool below, Air France bussed us to the old terminal. Two hours after landing we retrieved them from the single, overloaded carousel. People were crying and joking as though a war had started. A young black porter commented: 'Some architects don't know their ass, man.' Even in LA, dreamers flunk and buildings flood.

Carey's and my second book together aims to capture the special spirit of place to be found within three hours' freeway cruise of the Hollywood Hills — desert, mountain, ocean, city, and a melting-pot of nationalities and races at every level of society.

As a foreign visitor I have only recently begun to feel

WEST HOLLYWOOD FROM NORTH SELMA DRIVE

at home. It takes perseverance. They say, two years of it. First visit, you hate the place; second, you stay for life.

First visit, I was here to write a screenplay. It is a time-honoured screenwriter's bleat that his name is as well known to the public as the clapperboy's. I instantly tried to put this right by having a friend call me, at frequent intervals by the Beverly Hills Hotel pool, so my name would be continually requested over the pool's paging system. Everybody asked who I was. Nobody even offered me a job, let alone better billing.

But I did have Chinese food cooked by Danny Kaye; listen to a high-and-happy Jack Lemmon sing skat at a party; partner Janet Leigh of *Psycho* fame; and eavesdrop deals in the dinge of the Polo Lounge.

It is a small world. You're always bumping into people you don't know; and one or two you do — from Europe, New York, the past, yesterday's breakfast or tomorrow's script conference. But this small world is circumscribed by another huge one — Greater Los Angeles. On later visits my world expanded as, in trepidation, I made my first legal right turn on a red light (which Woody Allen claims to be LA's only contribution to culture), and headed for the Santa Monica Freeway — the big, wide world where movement is a constant high. Away from the claustro-

phobic confines of showbiz towards the Californian dreamscape of which that is only a part. In the local argot, I began to relate to the place. I really did. Really. I could handle it.

Camilla was living then in a charming house, overlooking a tree-lined, no-car pathway, two blocks from the beach at Venice. Her end of the street was middle-class bohemian but, contrary to most seaside real estate, the nearer the beach the rougher the property. On my way to swim I passed a ramshackle house from which wafted the smell of *tortillas* and the sound of *mariachi* music; bare-bottomed Mexican *chicos* erupted around an old heap of Oldsmobile, its hood permanently open with Papa and six *amigos* trying to fix it.

I took an instant liking to Venice, its louche boardwalk, shiny black skin in mini swimsuits, acrobatic skaters, mime artists, wild clothes on straight people, wilder clothes on gay people, good jazz, good tempers, the roar of surf and the smell of hash.

Later, Camilla moved to higher ground — a few feet above Strip level. To be above Sunset Strip was definitely a step up from Venice. Upward mobility can mean literally heading for the hills — Palos Verdes, Pacific Palisades and Mulholland Drive, looking down on that forever land of palm-tree suburbia known flatly as The Flats.

VENICE SKATER

But a Californian bungalow in the eternal spring of the LA Flats is a dream to many a person in its windy Chicago equivalent. Midwesterners wester towards the sunshine with confidence — that wonderful American ability to re-root. Strangers get to feel at home here, because it is a city of strangers.

It welcomes all comers with a sense of adventure. 'Have fun!' says the car-rental girl. 'Are you happy?' asks the air stewardess. Says the bank manager when you want to borrow a hundred grand to turn into your first million: 'Why not?' It is the land of positive thinking. Mere hope is just too dumb a concept. Not somewhere over the rainbow, but right here, right now in LA, dreams really do come true.

This is the dream of the dream, of course. Besides the Superhaves, the Superhavenots cast their shadow. Not too close, for fear of spoiling that eternal sunshine. Middle Americans, more than half the Angelenos, make a habit of not going bankrupt more than the okay twice — third time, forget it! The top five per cent, changing Rollses like diapers, don't even know the meaning of the word. Nor do the bottom forty per cent to whom bankruptcy has become the norm: blacks, Latinos, Downtown drug addicts — as opposed to those who use their knives to do coke in fashionable restaurants.

This is only part of the reality, the wake-up and disillusion expressed so poignantly by Chandler. A burned-out playboy in *The Long Goodbye* says: 'I'm rich — who the hell wants to be happy?'

The other part is that hicks from the sticks (as the envious call them) really do make it, become Beautiful People, clones of Joan Collins and Robert Redford, and the Gold Rush perpetuates its own myth.

Everything is available to those with nouse, balls and bizzazz. In life, unto death. It is super-sentimental, hyper-hedonistic — the land of the credit-card blowjob and the dead pet in a satin-lined casket. It is also a city of quiet people, minding their own business in exotic gardens, leading blameless lives in endless shopping malls. A city of pioneers — architecture, aerospace, entertainment, technology. LA's whirlwind history throws up a rich contrast in images for the photographer, shocks for the writer. Holdback is seldom in the picture; it's all go go go. From the TV studios to the hang-gliding to the yoga to the dietetic shop to the divorce lawyer, and back to Burbank, down to Malibu, to Palm Springs (your plane or mine?), to polo in Griffith Park, constantly on the move in a state of upward mobility.

It is exhilarating if you can stay the pace. The fairy tales beat Disneyland — and a few of them are for real.

JULIAN MORE, West Hollywood 1985

MALIBU DIVER

'Where the sun shines, the soul expands' is an old Spanish proverb. Eighteenth-century Spaniards sent forty-four peons from their Mexican colony to found the Californian settlement, naming it religiously El Pueblo de la Reina de Los Angeles de Porciúncula (Our Lady Queen of the Angels of Porciúncula). Sun in every syllable, though it wasn't exactly souls that expanded over the next two centuries. As the village of forty-four grew to the megalopolis of thirteen million, its flamboyant name shrunk with each sun-dreamy occupier. El Pueblo de Los Angeles for the post-Revolution Mexicans; just plain Los Angeles for the Yankee invaders; and now simply LA for all us international California dreamers, westering towards some mythic sunset from the dark ages. In those two magic initials, easily pronounceable for even the dumbest of us, each sees the dream of expansion he cherishes most.

Actors dream of becoming President. Trappist monks dream of having a TV chat show. And I dream not of expanding but slimming: if only I could look like that golden youth who skips to Vivaldi on the patio of his thatched Cotswold cottage with lemons round the door. 'Happy Christmas,' he wishes .me, laid-back between two skips, his jogging suit lemon to match the fruit and his Ferrari.

In the hot sun of Christmas, I eat Szechuan dumplings at a sidewalk café called Chin Chin next to a high-tech ice cream parlor on Sunset Plaza Drive. A giant *Cage Aux Folles* poster looms above a fine art shop with a Virgin Mary shrine in kitsch plaster – the nearest thing this Christmas to Our Lady Queen of the Angels of Porciúncula.

Hedonistic Christmas in this land of eternal summer (my dreambook tells me). I float from the cloudless blue of Santa Monica Boulevard into the Arrow

FATHER CHRISTMAS, VENICE BOARDWALK

SANTA CLAUS BOULEVARD

ing, group therapy, skating, carol-singing, hunting, water-skiing, party-going, seminars, golf, or reading the book I found in the trashcan. To swim in the desert and ski on a mountain, both on the same day. No wonder TV viewing is on the decline.

Long before TV ratings bothered anyone's sleep, novice Angelenos of the thirties arrived with high hopes. Humorist and Marx Brothers screenwriter S. J. Perelman recalls: 'And so, across the silver steppes amid the howling of wolves, we rode into a new destiny, purified in the crucible that men call Hollywood.' Was it the famed sunset he saw? No. 'In the distance a glow of huge piles of burning motion-picture scripts lit up the sky. The crisp tang of frying writers and directors whetted my appetite.' (*Strictly From Hunger*)

New York poetess Dorothy Parker, that Hollywood dissenter, loved the screenplay money, hated the place, and kept commuting by *two* glamorous trains (The Twentieth Century and Santa Fe Superchief) between 'Out Here', as the rootless call it, and her farm in Pennsylvania. A three-day commute each way, Anita Loos, of *Gentlemen Prefer Blondes* fame, tells us the Hollywood in-crowd left the train at the penultimate stop of Pasadena to avoid the hassle of fans and photographers at Union Station.

Supermarket and bump into old friends from London buying their low-fat turkey. A cool, casual meeting. 'The traveller takes himself wherever he goes,' Montaigne has it; on the contrary, here in LA, I am the open traveller, ready for a change from stuffy old Europe, ready to go with the dream where Santa Claus is feminine like Santa Barbara. And even the reindeer on Santa Claus Boulevard may be gay.

My dreambook also tells me money buys freedom. Freedom, over Christmas, to choose between free-falling, polo-playing, barbecueing, surfing, sunbath-

UNION STATION

SANTA MONICA MOUNTAINS

Aldous Huxley waxes more lyrical, as he views LA from the air in *Ape and Essence.*

> More oranges than anywhere,
> With bigger and better girls –
> The great metrollopis of the West.

El Dorado or Babylon? Or a bit of both? An early rancher could travel two days on horseback without leaving his land. It was blessed and hallowed land whose promises colonial dreamers pounced upon with energetic rapacity. In 1542 Portuguese explorer Cabrillo encountered the Shoshone Indians at their village of Yang-Na. Two centuries later Captain de Portolá annexed the land for Spain and, in 1771, the San Gabriel Mission was founded. With dire results for the Indians.

A note of irony rings from the mission bell of San Juan Capistrano where a plaque proclaims the Spanish intent to 'Christianize and civilize the Indians'.

A VIEW FROM THE HOLLYWOOD HILLS

SANTA BARBARA MISSION

BULLOCKS STORE

Within one hundred years they were all but extinct.

From early Catholic days to today's 'head trips', California dreamers have reconciled belief in themselves with belief in God, greed with gurus, and soul-expansion with getting the first million. Having their angel cake and eating it.

'God's great blueprint for man's abode on earth' was how Aimee Semple McPherson, twenties' faith healer, saw LA. Terminal cases flocked to the sunshine with dreams of recovery. 'Who will lay the foundations of my home?' cried Aimee at her prayer-meetings, turning spiritual healing into a personal bonanza and sending a few psychosomatics home happy. The laying-on-of-hands became the dipping-of-hands-into-pockets to finance Aimee's 'House That God Built'. She was the cult heroine *par excellence*.

Cults are big money, and none more so than the cult of death. Forest Lawn has this major plus: it is the only truly quiet spot in Los Angeles. Despite the bright and breezy TV commercial: 'If you want to end up in a nice low-price Forest Lawn cemetery, you'd better start off in a nice low-price Forest Lawn mortuary. Otherwise, who knows where you'll end up.'

The LA death wish no doubt came with the Mexicans. I once sat by mistake on a sugar skull marked 'Julian' from a Mexican Day of the Dead

ACUPRESSURE ON VENICE BEACH

FOREST LAWN MEMORIAL PARK

LA as a city where anything goes, any dream can be bought.

As the Eagles sang it in 1976:

There she stood in the doorway;
I heard the mission bell
And I was thinking to myself,
'This could be Heaven or this could be Hell'
Then she lit up a candle and she showed me the
way
There were voices down the corridor,
I thought I heard them say . . .

Welcome to the Hotel California
Such a lovely place (such a lovely face)
Plenty of room at the Hotel California
Any time of year, you can find it here.

Heaven or Hell? There has always been a sexual ambiguity about the city and the dreams it spins. Especially where Hollywood is concerned. As early as 1919, DeMille was making daring comedies about high life with titles like *Scrambled Wives* and *Her Purchase Price* – before discovering that the Bible packed audiences in tighter than Sin.

The seventies were bigtime for pornos: *Deep Throat*

fiesta; several years' bad luck followed. Nothing but good fortune, however, came to Los Angeles from the Mexican defeat of the Spaniards in 1822, death wish or not. Post-revolution LA saw the lush life of the *ranchos*, grandees trading hide with the Yankees in return for silks to clothe their *señoras*.

It was a *Dolce Vita* existence, both elegant and wild, with Indian servants for the Mexican *rancheros*, and Indian whores for the Yankee traders. Olvera Street, LA's oldest thoroughfare, jumped with grogshops, gambling dens and brothels. It began the tradition of

JESUS COMES TO VENICE

grossed $3,200,000. And Hollywood's reputation for lack of balls disappeared on the bandwagon of permissiveness. I recently saw a re-run of *Bob and Carol and Ted and Alice* (1969), Paul Mazursky's witty comedy of manners about LA's Swinging Sixties wife-swapping morality. Two uptight, pretentious couples play at being hip, dreaming of liberation at Esalen encounter groups. But when it comes to four-in-a-bed they flunk.

In a TV discussion afterwards with the film's makers

and actors, Mazursky said his studio had turned it down as a dirty idea; if he could get Paul Newman and Joanne Woodward, it would of course be cleaner. Elliott Gould confessed to wearing two pairs of underpants for the orgy sequence. Mazursky made the point that his characters were not jet-set, they were typical middle-class Angelenos ('heroic America') and their failure to wife-swap was not a cop-out. In fact, the cop-out label came from New York critics who, in Mazursky's view, are always way behind. What is current on the Coast, Madison Avenue gets round to four years later. One of LA's favourite dreams, that.

Cop-out or not, the confusion of those touchingly absurd couples seems as relevant today as it was then. And totally representative of a morality which censors Shakespeare textbooks but lets TV violence run riot. Its vocal majority is far too puritan to let LA become the sleazeville its knockers claim it to be. After playing Babylon, it takes off its whore's make-up and reverts to Babbittown. With dreams of Debbie Reynolds instead of Linda Lovelace.

Periodic clean-ups are milestones of LA's history. The first followed the US defeat of the Mexicans in 1848. A year later the Gold Rush up north made LA rich by providing the forty-niners with good red meat

PLAYMATE PROMOTION ON HOLLYWOOD BOULEVARD

to keep them digging. LA beef-farmers were the original flash Angelenos, with silver-mounted saddles so heavy their horses collapsed under the weight. The newly-arrived Yankees also got rich from servicing the cattle boomtown with stage-coaches, gambling saloons, and liquor.

After the financial clean-up came the clean-up of morals. With the arrival of puritan midwestern opportunists over the next forty years, it was the only time souls expanded as fast as the city.

Jesus Saves – And So Should You at the Pacific Ten-Cent Bank!

General Harrison Gray Otis, founder of the *Los Angeles Times*, wanted for his city 'Workers, hustlers, men of brawn and grit, capitalists who seek large returns on honest transactions'. He did not want 'Dudes, loafers, paupers . . . people too near to death to be saved by anything but a miracle'.

His future son-in-law, Harry Chandler, arrived in LA with tuberculosis, sensibly kicked it, and became a millionaire – far richer than Otis by merely *distributing* the *LA Times*. He was the first middle-man baron, marrying the boss's daughter and riding local politicians with the deftness of a surfer on a barrelling breaker.

Otis and Chandler were the ancestors of *Dynasty*.

Whereas Harry Gaylord Wilshire was of wilder stuff, both as a millionaire and dead broke. Chasing the quick buck, he was a subdivider of land, swindler, socialist candidate, banker, inventor, gold-mine owner, publisher and lecturer. Not bad for a Harvard man. In 1925 he invented a Monty Python-esque machine that claimed to turn grey hair black, make women's hair curly, and cure cancer into the bargain. He died before anyone could sue him, leaving 15-mile long, 120-foot wide Wilshire Boulevard as a monument to his broad ambitions.

CHRISTMAS, BEVERLY HILLS

WILSHIRE BOULEVARD

These early, larger-than-life Angeleno opportunists inspired later writers to dream up a few dreamers of their own. Budd Schulberg, in 1941, created Sammy Glick as the classic Hollywood anti-hero and was accused, ridiculously, of being an anti-Semitic Jew. Brooklyn-born Sammy of *What Makes Sammy Run?* comes 'sprinting out of his mother's womb, turning life into a race in which the only rules are fight for the rail, and elbow on the turn, and the only finish-line is death'. Messenger in a New York newspaper office, Sammy dreams of becoming a Hollywood mogul and using 'dough for wallpaper'. His motto is: 'If you can't be smart, be loud.'

More romantic than the hard-nosed Sammy is Monroe Stahr, F. Scott Fitzgerald's movie-mogul hero of his unfinished novel *The Last Tycoon*. Fitzgerald's movie people are human beings, not grotesques. Workaholic widower Stahr, searching for the likeness of his adored dead wife, believes he has found the remake in an English girl, Kathleen. Kathleen first floats towards him on a huge prop head of the Hindu God Shiva, dislodged in the flooding of a studio backlot after an earthquake. This wonderful, surreal image is quintessential LA – and makes me all the more eager for Fellini's long-awaited Hollywood movie.

Fitzgerald, even at his most self-mocking in the Pat Hobby stories (confessions of a washed-up Hollywood hack), is upbeat about LA. In a sense, it gave him 'the right angle, that dearest of Hollywood dreams'. From alcoholic crack-up and literary extinction, he rose briefly from the ashes to pen screenplays, including one for Shirley Temple whom he considered very bright. It paid for daughter Scottie's Vassar education, wife Zelda's sanitorium, and helped pave the way to his regained reputation in American literature, albeit after his death.

Far more important than the binges and blood-letting and gossip-column myth-making is what he actually wrote. Stahr's words about LA might be referring to their author: ' . . . it was everyone's secret that sustained effort was difficult here – a secret that Stahr scarcely admitted to himself. But he knew that people from other places spurted a pure rill of new energy for a while.'

For a while, Fitzgerald had joined the sober dreamers whose only intoxication is the place itself. A high of opportunity. The sober dreamers flocked for the agriculture, dashed for the oil, moved in on the movies. Call it enterprise or avarice, for whatever reason the luck of others spurred them on to fight for a bit of The Big Orange. If not a whole orange grove.

UNIVERSAL STUDIOS

THE BEL AIR HOTEL

Biggest landowner in 1868, Don Abel Stearns (his very name a mix of Hispanic Catholicism, Jewish chutzpah and Bible Belt straightlacedness) sold his seven ranches to a land development company. He was the first of the men to promote LA – they were known as boosters. And the first realtor, Robert M. Widney, of Ohio, sold cheap subdivisions to the flood of Middle West immigrants.

The soul-expanders of Kansas, punching Bibles instead of faces, replaced the frontier-town honky-tonks with Presbyterian churches. Sun mellowed the stern midwesterners, as wheat-farmers turned to vines, olives and citrus fruits.

LA's few remaining Victorian buildings owe much to this mellowing. There is a jolliness about their 'Steamboat Gothic' style: high pointed gables, flamboyant shinglework, balconies where the fancy took them.

In 1887, a little old lady bought a subdivision of Pasadena for $50 before lunch and sold it for $200 after lunch. Given that this was before fast food and the lunch could have lasted a good hour, figure out what that land will be worth in 1987. And you know why realtors are still dream-spinning. Not to mention the attendant masons, plumbers, Japanese gardeners, poolmen, paper-hangers, and every ilk of trend-setter.

If your interior decorator tells you everyone is into beaten brass this year, you cannot afford to be without beaten brass all over the house. Even if you can't afford it.

Whatever your income and size of dream, LA has always been good at the hard sell. Boosters milked their golden cow for every last drop. Their dreams of expansion were eminently practical. In 1892 Henry Huntington, doyen of the railroad fortunes, linked Downtown Los Angeles to the sea with his twenty-one-mile Pacific Electric Railway. The big red cars

TWO BEVERLY HILLS STATUES

POOLSIDE, CRESCENT HEIGHTS

TOM IN THE POOL, OUTPOST DRIVE

rattled along at fifty-five mph, the speed limit of today's freeways, and did the journey in half the time of today's buses. The same year, Edward L. Doheny struck oil; and Mrs Summers, a piano teacher, became Oil Queen of California. A wooden derrick in your back garden was a status symbol.

Booster dreams ended with the Depression, when further immigrants, escaping in beat-up cars from the dust-bowl, were headed off at the pass with armed force. Now it was the turn of the movies to spin the dreams – an escape from harsh realities.

A good escapist movie resembles LA itself: a dream, but, however implausible, its images and characters are identifiable. It demands a gut response. And, by

providing what the public wanted, the motion-picture industry grew as fast and haphazardly as the city.

It all began way back in 1907. Fleeing bad weather on Lake Michigan, Francis Boggs, director of the Selig Company, had continued shooting *The Count Of Monte Cristo* in LA. As it was too costly to bring his Chicago actors, Boggs hired look-alike locals and disguised them. When one lost his wig after being hit by a big wave, Boggs was more concerned to save the wig than the actor. Actors came cheap in the spontaneous, boosterless migration to the newly appointed suburb called Hollywood.

The rest, as they say in the movies, is history.

Dream palaces sprouted on the Hollywood Hills like chaparral. Tod Hackett, hero of Nathanael West's *The Day of the Locust*, is fascinated by 'Mexican ranch houses, Samoan huts, Mediterranean villas, Egyptian and Japanese temples, Swiss chalets, Tudor cottages, and every combination of these styles'. The grosser the better.

Valentino built Falcon Lair, his dream palace with solid sixteenth-century Florentine doors, private gasoline tank for his Isotta Fraschini, and a pack of killer guard-dogs to maul marauding females. Douglas Fairbanks and Mary Pickford entertained European royalty at Pickfair, a Stockbroker Tudor mansion

ART DECO APARTMENTS, WEST HOLLYWOOD

where, in terror of egghead visitors like Einstein and H. G. Wells, they showed movies to avoid conversation. Harold Lloyd's Greenacres was most grandiose: forty bedrooms, nine-hole golf course, and 800-foot canoeing pond; Harold and his wife found the elevator the cosiest place; his Christmas tree took so long to decorate, it stayed up all year round.

Way below those eyries de luxe, lesser dreamers got their 'Film Fantasy' kicks, eating at the Brown Derby (hat-shaped) and the Tail o' the Pup (tail-o'-the-pup shaped); and visiting the picture palaces of the Broadway. Best and least-known tourist attraction in LA, this stunning tour of the Broadway theatre district is organized by the energetic and much-needed Los Angeles Conservancy. Still extant are the Roxy, Cameo, Palace, Globe, Tower, Rialto, Orpheum, Loew's State.

At the Los Angeles Theater there were bread-lines on the sidewalk as the stars arrived for the première of Chaplin's *City Lights*. For twenty-five cents' admission you shared the luxury with the stars.

The dream begins as you enter — crystal chandeliers, baroque mirrors, fountains, tapestries. Besides the

genuine opulence, there is impeccable service. Children's playroom, dancing, restaurants, writing room with headed paper, electric cigarette lighters in panelled walls, a primitive monitoring system to view the movie in the lobby. And the Ladies' Rest Room, fit for Queen or First Lady (of screen or country) — has individual marble-and-brass, air-conditioned cubicles worthy of a Ritz, special mirrors to check the back of your dress, and maids to do your hair. There is even a crying room for upset children.

When I visited, I was greeted by the pervasive smell of popcorn, the sound of Spanish, and the sight of a girl on screen stripping naked in front of a Mexican cop. For the Broadway theatres are now an entirely Latino movie preserve — but preserved they are, thank God. No one should miss the Spanish Gothic cathedral decor — personal taste of Mary Pickford at her United Artists Theater; its cherubs have the faces of UA executives.

The Broadway on a Saturday morning, bustling with entirely Third World and mostly Latino life, is typical of LA's dreamscape. I love its jazzy muddle of styles. It has a brash, high-spirited gutsiness lacking in Europe's great cities.

MURAL OF THE STARS, HOLLYWOOD BOULEVARD

STANDUP COMICS' THEATRE, SUNSET STRIP

Europeans relish its openness. Over the years they have pursued LA dreams in their escape from persecution, a hide-bound class structure, or lack of opportunity. Daily you bump into a budding British rock artiste waiting on table till the big break, a Hungarian director who left his country in 1956, an Italian architect with a dream house somebody here can actually pay for. LA is a club only restricted by lack of cash; anyone reasonably legal is welcome to the dream.

Europeans are at home in what Noël Coward described as 'a sort of disreputable senility'. It is both over-ripe and under-aged, like someone in second childhood; much of LA seems to have been there a lot longer than it actually has. As Raymond Chandler evokes it in *The Big Sleep*, describing a beach gambling club: 'It was now a big, dark, outwardly shabby place in a thick grove of wind-twisted Monterey cypresses, which gave it its name. It had enormous scrolled porches, turrets all over the place, stained-glass trims around the big windows, big, empty stables at the back, a general air of nostalgic decay.'

I cherish dreams of the past as unlikely as an encounter in a game of Consequences: Bertolt Brecht playing open-air chess in Washington Square; Luis Buñuel writing gags for Chaplin; a Hollywood hostess saying to avant-garde composer Schoenberg, originator of the twelve-note scale: 'Give us a tune, Arnold.'

Igor Stravinsky, Thomas Mann, André Malraux, Aldous Huxley – LA Europeans were doing a Henry James in reverse, bringing their culture with them and finding it a good visiting card. The origins of the Men Who Made Hollywood are too well known to repeat here, but the Sammy Glicks needed the intellectuals and the Romanoffs to give them the veneer that fitted their image of themselves. So, in the wake of the rough diamonds who spun the dreams for the plebs,

LIBERACE'S POOL BAR

came Europeans to spin dreams for the moguls and stars — architects, interior decorators and vocal coaches. Bogus Russian princes ran restaurants and out-of-work British actors taught you how to talk proper. At a price.

The Brits settled in best because, having no gastronomy of their own, they could easily adjust to California's. They created their own type-cast dream world: the cricket team of C. Aubrey Smith (colonel type); the japes of David Niven (adventurer type); the drawl of George Sanders (cad type); and a man called Pratt (monster type), who changed his name to Boris Karloff. The most Anglo-Saxon of them all in appearance, Leslie Howard, was in fact a Jew so orthodox he refused to shoot a foot of film on the sabbath.

It was a pleasant, leisured life of not so much a colony, as Evelyn Waugh fictionalized it, as a number of cliques. Rather more like Potters Bar than Poona. Today tradition dies hard with Britain still batting a strong team: Joan Collins, Dudley Moore, Tony Richardson, Malcolm McDowell; not forgetting our great star the *Queen Mary*, docked in magnificent absurdity as a hotel-cum-tourist attraction. The Art Deco bar is worth the trip to Long Beach.

But for foreigners LA is not just a British hunting ground. I recently met a Frenchman from Cairanne,

the next village to mine in Vaucluse. The coincidence was to be expected; there are no coincidences in dreams. René runs Du Vin, a charming wineshop on San Vicente. 'People in Beverly Hills like to be seen drinking French,' he explained. Was it because Californian Chardonnay was usually more expensive on restaurant wine-lists? Not a bit. A Sancerre or Brouilly was just more in line with the cosmopolitan dream — like a BMW or Yves St-Laurent.

Or Disneyland? Here you can tour the world of your dreams with no more trouble than a freeway crawl to Orange County. Says the brochure: 'Board an explorer's launch to venture down dangerous tropical rivers and penetrate the jungle.' 'Race through icy caverns towards an encounter with the Abominable Snowman!' 'Fly over London to Never Land (sic) aboard a pirate galleon.' From the Peter Pan Flight to the Mark Twain Steamboat via the Mission to Mars, Disneyland is a tribute to LA mobility.

At one spot I could see submarines, cable-cars, a monorail, racing cars, a bobsleigh on the Matterhorn, speedboats, and an overhead tramway called a PeopleMover. And the only risk in all this journeying is losing your child or your car. Facilities for retrieving children are catered for by the Carefree

DISNEYLAND, ANAHEIM

WATTS MURAL

Staff, but you may never find your car again in those vast wastes of former orange grove converted into a mega-carpark. Without it, you're lost. A freeway derelict.

It is an LA habit to knock the freeway. Don't. It is a vital part of the leisure dream. Its very name is a metaphor: free way. Myself, I prefer its slow speeds and lack of competitiveness to the slaughterous, Grand Prix tailgating of French autoroutes. Often attractive to the eye, even within LA's hundred-city conurbation, the freeway surprises with distant views of blue mountains or surf-flecked ocean or seven bank buildings rising reassuringly from tropical foliage.

The freeway has become part of Pop Art folklore, like Coke cans and customized cars. Along the Ventura are murals by the LA Fine Arts Squad. Murals like 'The Isle Of California' off Santa Monica Boulevard, showing an apocalyptic nightmare of a freeway's cliffhanging end after some ecological disaster. Not all are so doom-laden. In Watts, vivid murals express the dreams of the black community; they depict Martin Luther King, Stevie Wonder, and other inspirational figures who have made it out of the ghetto.

Or there is the marvel of Watts Towers, Simon Rodia's architectural firework display in pottery and metal. His naïve, thirty-three-year dream tempts comparison with Gaudi or Facteur Cheval's house. But Reyner Banham, brilliant essayist on LA's architectural wonders, rates Italian tile-setter Rodia's towers truly original.

'. . . in his determination to "do something big" and in his ability to walk away when they were finished in 1954, Rodia was very much at one with the surfers, hot-rodders, sky-divers, and scuba-divers who personify the tradition of private, mechanistic *satori*-seeking in California.' (*Los Angeles: The Four Ecologies*)

Typical of the do-your-own-thing culture. Although the business community has been generous in its large-scale sponsorship of the arts (Ahmanson, Chandler, Norton Simon, Getty), LA lacks a cultural centre. Music lovers tend to form community symphony orchestras at the drop of a baton; weekend artists get painter's elbow; the abundance of writers' conferences precludes the necessity of actually writing.

Dreams of cultural heritage may have remained dreams, but LA is far from 'the plastic ass-hole of the

WATTS TOWERS

JAGUAR BILLBOARD, HOLLYWOOD HILLS

world' that William Faulkner described. Raymond Chandler, nostalgic though he was for London literary life, had deep affection for LA's leisurely past. In *The Little Sister* he has Philip Marlowe say this about it: 'I used to like this town. There were trees along Wilshire Boulevard. Beverly Hills was a country town . . . Hollywood was a bunch of frame houses . . . Los Angeles was a big, dry, sunny place with ugly houses and no style, but good-hearted and friendly. It had the climate they yap about now. People used to sleep out on porches. Little groups who thought they were intellectual used to call it the Athens of America. It wasn't that, but it wasn't a neon-lighted slum either.'

And to this very day, not five minutes above Sunset Strip, a friend picks his own untreated oranges for juice, his garden rampages with bougainvillaea and hibiscus, his barbecued Pacific prawns still taste of the ocean.

Dream food and drink abound. Perelman recalls 'a duplexburger and a Giant Malted Milk Too Thick for a Straw.' He meets a copywriter getting 'the right poetic throb' for Mother Stentorian's Fish Kebabs: ' . . . they are portioned into appetizing, mouth-sized chunks, sprinkled with mace, dill, rape, capsicum and rose leaves, and pre-cooked on skewers over aromatic fires of specially processed driftwood imported from far-away Armenia . . . these fishliks are impregnated with the songs of Asia Minor.' (*Genuflection in the Sun*)

My own gastronomic experience includes a mosque-like Arabian restaurant where a *djellaba*-wearing waiter, with fair hair flowing from his *fez*, announced in the sweet tones of LA waiterdom: 'Hi, I'm Larry and I shall shortly be washing your hands in rose-water, prior to serving your traditional Moroccan feast.' After the feast, we were entertained by a luscious belly-dancer.

Dashing between one navel-swinging gig and another, she kindly gave me a lift to a business appointment I was late for. I heard how her drama coach and numerologist were helping her to be less flaky. And how liberating it was for a Jewish girl from Dallas to be a belly dancer in an Arab restaurant; they should try it in Jerusalem.

I have also chased a cork ring, keeping my Jumbo Margarita afloat, down the waterfall between two landscaped pools. Without losing the paper parasol.

It was like chasing a dream down Sunset Boulevard. You must catch it. This is Middle America, where a truck driver can earn more than a bank vice-president. And all I have to say, to catch that dream, is: 'I wouldn't dream of losing.' Whether at polo or self-promotion, losing is the only impossible dream.

SUSHI BAR, LA CIENEGA BOULEVARD

DAWN ON THE HOLLYWOOD HILLS

DAWN ON SUNSET STRIP

REALITY

Do you know the way to San José?

So sang Dionne Warwick in Hal David's mordant lyric of The Big Awakening, the onset of *heimweh*, that longing for home and friends — only just up the coast in San José but far enough from grim reality.

LA takes you up, and lets you down. A gentle let-down, maybe. From San José or Denver, Manchester or Melbourne, come young hopefuls to the mythic freeway, where LA promises the ride that will make them stars. With the exhilaration of arrival, no one ever doubts they will be a star, whether of screen, rag trade or real estate. No one, not for one tiny, heretical minute, would dare to think the unthinkable: in two years time, they'll still be parking cars or waiting on table. But many are doing just that — if they have not, like the girl in the song, given up and gone home.

On the sixties' rock scene, beefs were also expressed with rip-roaring, banjo-strumming abandon by the incomparable Mamas and Papas, delivering 'Creeque Alley'.

We can't go on indefinitely,
And California dreaming
Is becoming a reality. . .

In LA — you know where that's at,
Everyone's gettin' fat
Except Mama Cass.

Ironical that songs of struggle and disillusion made their singers, composers and lyricists rich. Tunes to these laments were defiantly happy; I cannot imagine Brecht, uneasy exile from Nazi Germany, allowing Kurt Weill to come up with any melody that was not sour as a Hollywood lemon. Faced with its realities, Brecht ceased to use America as a setting for his songs and plays: his only theatrical achievement in LA was Joe Losey's production of *Galileo* in 1947.

LA CIENEGA BOULEVARD

THE ROSE BOWL MARKET, PASADENA

Appropriate, however, that LA should have premiered a play about a scientist at that time. After World War II came the rise of the aerospace, electronics, and highly sophisticated armaments industries. With the Vietnam War came that rude awakening, the realization that the American Dream wasn't all it was cracked up to be. LA was comparatively close to Vietnam; after Pearl Harbor, it was its second traumatic encounter with the Pacific rim. Boats and planes left with men and munitions; they returned with the coffins. Ordinary Angelenos became critical and questioning of their society, with a disillusion previously left to the writers and, more rarely, movie-makers.

In *The Day of the Locust* Nathanael West's schizophrenic wage-slaves dream of leisured futures that elude them. An ambitious starlet and her ex-comedian father are still selling silver polish door-to-door. A silent movie actress is now a Madame. A female tennis champ has 'a pretty, eighteen-year-old face and thirty-five-year-old neck that was veined and sinewy'. A man imagines himself to look like a portly Southern colonel, whereas he's hunched and dessicated. When they realize they have been conned by the dream, their fury flares into riotous revenge at a phony Mardi Gras.

West's hero, Tod Hackett, though glutted with sunsets, surf and orange juice, somehow manages to retain his compassion: 'It is hard to laugh at the need for beauty and romance, no matter how tasteless, however horrible the results of that need are. But it is easy to sigh. Few things are sadder than the truly monstrous.' A dwarf in a Tyrolean hat on Hollywood Boulevard; a life-like 'dead' rubber horse at the bottom of a swimming pool; the soulless blockhouse pretentiously called The San Bernardino Arms where Hackett lives.

BLONDE IN A ROLLS, BEVERLY HILLS

In the literature of LA, however, it is not just tough at the bottom.

Even the hyper-successful Sammy Glick, running on a full tank of his own gas, gets his come-uppance, cheated on at his very moment of glory by his socialite wife. 'Sometimes I think the three chief products this town turns out are moving pictures, ambition and fear.'

In the city of has-beens, Marion Davies remained a never-was. One of the most attractive of LA hostesses, generous and funny, Marion called her press baron lover, William Randolph Hearst, 'droopy drawers'. But that old paramour's maddening interference with her promising movie career kept her firmly in her place: socially at the top, artistically at the bottom – a mere model for Orson Welles's off-key opera singer in *Citizen Kane*.

Marion did not need social security. Whereas Dorothy Parker, on her last Coast stint, alcoholic and broke, lived on Norma Place, a far cry from her previous butler-and-Bollinger incarnation. She was, however, handy for the Unemployment Compensation Office, and not the least ashamed of picking up her $600 monthly check – along with Marlon Brando, arriving in his Rolls.

When all else fails and if you don't fancy that walk into the waves from Venice beach, there is always the Arroyo Seco Bridge in Pasadena, which claimed seventy-nine suicides in the thirties. Or do the thing like a British gentleman when fired by his studio. As though drummed out of his regiment, Evelyn Waugh's Sir Francis Hinsley earns this funeral ode.

> They told me, Francis Hinsley, they told me you were hung
> With red protruding eye-balls and black protruding tongue
> I wept as I remembered how often you and I
> Had laughed about Los Angeles and now 'tis here you'll lie;
> Here pickled in formaldehyde and painted like a whore,
> Shrimp-pink incorruptible, not lost nor gone before.
>
> *(The Loved One)*

LA is a city of extremes: the higher you rise, the lower you fall. And the wilder you dream, the ruder the awakening.

It is partly to do with that deceptive climate. As a child in Wales, one of my great thrills was the second feature of double-bills, invariably a Hollywood gangster movie with a car chase. It always seemed to be

SUNSET BOULEVARD

SMOG OVER HOLLYWOOD

next to mine was twitched enough to grab my knee instead of the arm-rest.

Then there's the smog. A book on LA without smog would be like writing of Naples without Vesuvius. Owing to a set of special climatic conditions, LA gets lumbered with having invented the beastly stuff. Here's how: hot Pacific air moves in from ocean to city. Lower layer is cooled by cold coastal currents and mingles with hydrocarbon from cars and nitrogen oxide from factories. Warmer top layer is the lid on the grey soup tureen. With no wind, and the mountains forming a bowl, the smog has nowhere to go but lungs, eyes, plant life and, ironically, car tyres, causing them to crack.

raining too hard, as though the rain machine was at full pressure. In Llanelli, South Wales, though one of the wettest spots in the British Isles, we never had anything like that. But it was no exaggeration. Fitzgerald describes it as 'the sound of horses weeing'.

One November I landed at LAX in fog so dense we only saw the ground lights five seconds before touch-down. An airline pilot in the passenger seat

To be fair, killer smogs only do their worst in the hottest months; most of the year is relatively smog-free and controls have become stricter. But two-thirds of the pollution is caused by road transport. It is unrealistic to believe the city that pioneered smog will also pioneer a viable electric car; the oil and auto-mobile lobbies are too powerful. A fortune is spent on Star Wars, much less on preserving our world.

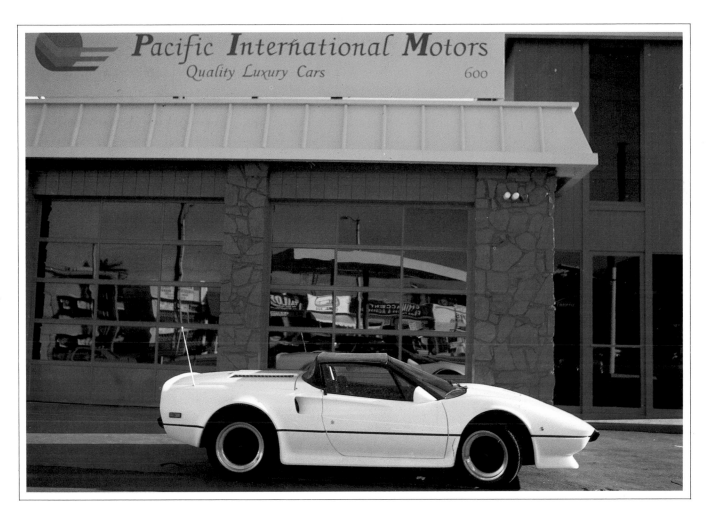

CAR SHOWROOM, MELROSE AVENUE

LA is not alone, of course. What major city is not polluted by its traffic? It just seems more poignant here. LA was once the orange-perfumed paradise of 'lungers' – sufferers from emphysema, bronchitis or asthma. By an ocean as romantic as the Pacific, when tall palms disappear into a grey-blue haze and the sun is invisible at eighty-seven degrees, my stinging eyes shed a tear or two for the quality of life.

Man-made hazards are one thing. LA must also cope with drought, fire and earthquake.

After terrible waterless years between 1892 and 1904, William Mulholland built his aqueduct to the city from Owens Valley beneath the High Sierras. The construction had all the drama of a Western: dynamiting by saboteurs, threats of lynching, corrupt politics, strong-arm tactics and the opening up of new territory to agriculture. Orchards flourished where there had been desert.

BURTON WAY, BEVERLY HILLS

And the high emotion of Californian water still exists today, nowhere better illustrated than in Roman Polanski's thriller, *Chinatown*, based on a true story. Men who control the water supply have a thumb on LA's jugular vein.

About earthquakes, Angelenos are much more laid-back, and precautions are astonishingly haphazard despite the evident danger. An ad for an upmarket housing development advertises itself with: 'Buy your dream house right on the San Andreas Fault. Guaranteed quake-proofing.' To be on the shelf is to be in the swim, a tremor during cocktails gives you a fearless image that can clinch a business deal. The last big one, in 1971, a mere 6.4 on the Richter scale, caused $553 million damages in one minute. Twenty cloverleaf overpasses collapsed. There were seventy deaths.

If not the tremor, the trauma of the 1985 Mexico City earthquake was deeply felt in East Los Angeles,

BEVERLY HILLS

TOPANGA CANYON AFTER FOREST FIRE

where many families had relatives who suffered. Emergency Relief Operation California was an instant expression of fellow feeling and action. It seems that it has to actually *happen*, before anyone takes much notice.

'We didn't get the full shock like at Long Beach, where the upper stories of shops were spewed into the streets and small hotels drifted out to sea – but for a full minute our bowels were one with the bowels of the earth – like some nightmare attempt to attach our navel cords again and jerk us back to the womb of creation.' (*The Last Tycoon*)

Like tigers burning bright, fires of chaparral leap and roar through the canyons and over the hills. Jumping hundreds of feet high across the fire-roads, they defy the firefighters and leave a desolate wasteland. Topanga Canyon looks like a battlefield after the flame-throwers have passed by. Perelman warns: 'Indian summer was nigh, with the promise of flaming color from the fires and mud slides in its canyons that annually draw thousands of tourists from Vermont.' (*Back Home in Tinseltown*)

He also warns of the dangers of cactus when searching for a doorbell in the dark. Finding any off-the-beaten-track address in LA risks forty days in the wilderness. Apart from the hour's freeway drive,

MALIBU BEACH

THE VALLEY

snapping at my privates; after setting off countless alarm systems to have James Bond heavies looming out of the dark with laser guns; after rending the hibiscus-and-chow-mein scented air with obscenities, we ended up in Malibu. When we did actually find the house, Carey swore it had mud-slid down the hill to another road. From the miniscule, rusty street-sign, I just wouldn't know. Anyway, the party was over.

So much for high life in the hills. When dawn comes crashing through my window on North Selma Drive, I look down beyond the dream giant posters of Sunset Strip, beyond the fairy-castle turrets of the Chateau Marmont to the realities of Slurb — God's Great Grid.

allow another for getting lost — even if you've been there before. After an hour, give up. Remember Garbo's advice about parties: never refuse, never go, no one misses anyone.

I once trailed Carey's car up Laurel Canyon, because she *knew* she knew the precise location of an imposing ranch-house just off Mulholland Drive which she'd visited many times. After reversing down dirt tracks amid the howling of wolves and Doberman pinschers

Slurb is short for sloppy, sleazy, slovenly, slip-shod urban. It is the huge mass of Greater Los Angeles. Seen from the air on a clear night, Slurb has a deceptive orderliness.

It implies a suburban outlook, and intellectual snobs from outside quite wrongly label Angelenos with this limitation. In fact, it is a cosmopolitan place, absorbing its many influences like a bold, anarchic mongrel.

MULHOLLAND DRIVE ABOVE THE VALLEY

THE WESTIN BONAVENTURE HOTEL, DOWNTOWN

DOWNTOWN LA

SUNSET BOULEVARD MANSION

Even the dingbat housing of the Flats expresses traditional Angeleno individuality by adding to the basic two-storey walk-up apartments a frontage of ethnic originality. So realtors describe them in ads as Tacoburger Aztec, Cod Cape Cod, Custom Chalet, Gourmet Mansardic or Polynesian Gabled.

Real Estate is all. Despite the disillusion with prices averaging $104,367 per home, persistent dreamers still manage to find their dream house.

A tract that attracts must have a suitable exotic name, often with absurd juxtapositions: Brittany Mountain, Gleneagles-in-the-Desert, Connemara Plaza or Rancho Jungfrau.

Modern realtor ads are poetry, written by the Ginsbergs and Ferlinghettis of commerce.

A FREE GOLF-CART with your $155,999 home at Highland Heights Country Club with solarium, wet bar, trash compactor, casual media lounge and spacious breakfast nook. AN EXCLUSIVE GUARD-GATED community with desert-style championship golf-course. Each home nestling on the fairway.

But sometimes things can go wrong. A rich building contractor built a dream house in secret for his wife. 'Darling,' he said when the house was ready for occupation, 'this Iranian has invited us to his house-warming tonight. Sorry, but we just have to go.' Thus had he organized a surprise house-warming for his wife. But when they got to the entrance, the wife exclaimed: 'My God, what a nouveau riche monstrosity!' The husband bravely banished his shattered ego, suggested a quiet dinner, left his house-warming guests cooling off, and sold the house to a genuine Iranian next day.

BEL AIR HOME

WATTS NURSERY SCHOOL

In Watts they do not have that kind of housing problem. A 1959 California State Law forbade discrimination in real estate, but lending institutions turned down prosperous blacks wishing to move from Watts into white areas. As in London and Paris, whites fear a black or brown face will reduce property values.

The difference between LA and Europe is not only the size of the problem, but the activist militancy of the sixties which brought the world's attention to it. Radical chic whites went to Black Panther fund-raising brunches; Black Panthers went, more importantly, to prison – or, like Eldridge Cleaver, abroad.

'Burn, Baby, Burn!' cried the Watts rioters in 1965. Thousands of blacks had come to LA in World War II to help with defence work and the aircraft industry. Many slept on park benches. Years later, their children were still living in an overcrowded ghetto, cut off from the city's main arteries with no adequate public transport system.

Black youths attacked respectable blacks on Central Avenue. Aggravated by the heat, it was a big bang from a long, slow-burning fuse of bitterness. The arrival of white cops, highway patrolmen, state troopers, city marshalls and firemen was the fuel on the fire. Over-reaction all round led to arson, looting, Molotov cocktails and drunken marauding. After five days the toll was 34 dead, 1,032 wounded.

Watts today does not have the congestion of Harlem, Brixton or Belleville. More people live in individual, two-storey homes in more space. Inhabitants have made much out of little by imaginative painting, and a sense of pride in their neighbourhood. Every year the Watts Summer Festival is held as a reminder of the riot's tragedy. Black youth found its own, more peaceful expression of individuality in break-dancing, mime, murals and sport. But no one

MARTIN LUTHER KING MURAL, WATTS

DERELICT RAILROAD STATION, WATTS

DEFIANCE AND RELIGION, WATTS

RODEO DRIVE, BEVERLY HILLS

should mistake safety-valves for a solution. A ghetto nihilism has replaced organized violence; with un-employment, as everywhere in the world, comes lassitude and despair.

Over the years, owing to its multiracial complexity, Los Angeles finds its white majority growing increasingly edgy. The classic Angeleno dichotomy between open-handed generosity and puritan up-tightness explodes occasionally into public or private violence against the outsider.

The insularity of the Chinese made them a natural target for Angeleno paranoia. In 1871 American workers agitated against Chinese 'cheap' labour. A policeman killed in a brawl near the Plaza led to a redneck attack on the *adobe* huts of the nearby Chinese quarter. The ensuing gun battle ended with the lynching of nineteen Chinese. The sheriff could not restore order without the help of ordinary citizens, and fearless realtor Robert M. Widney went into the fray, six-shooter blazing.

In 1943 Chicano girls in elaborate hairdos and zoot-suited youths clashed with US sailors in dance-halls. The sailors, taunted by the Chicanos, took revenge by going after them with clubs and black-jacks. This West Coast Story ended with no deaths but increased sourness from the Chicanos, whom the police blamed for the whole riot.

Thirty years later, LA's Chicano population was over one million, the biggest Mexican population outside Mexico City.

The Angeleno Establishment, in this city of mass aristocracy, is not so much anti-colour as anti-poor. Boosters like General Otis reckoned minorities should shape up or shut up. And until the Vietnam War, Angelenos espoused left-wing causes at their peril. Even Jewish film tycoons, pleading ignorance of Hitler's anti-Semitism, pounced heavily upon The Red

CHINATOWN TAXIDRIVER

Menace among their screenwriters and actors who urged anti-Nazi action.

Two political events did untold harm to fellow-travellers like Dorothy Parker: the Soviet-German pact during the war and the Cold War which followed it. Mean mouths said the nearest Parker had been to Russia was a plate of caviar. More seriously, anti-Soviet hysteria lead to the vicious witch-hunt by Senator McCarthy, which involved more than three hundred Hollywood employees. Of these, the courageous Unfriendly Ten Screenwriters took the 5th

WATCHING TV, BEVERLY WILSHIRE HOTEL

Amendment, refused to name names of suspected Communists (never an illegal party), and went to jail. Chaplin and Brecht were deported.

To this day, stepping out of line is bad news. The cautionary tale of John Belushi, as told by Bob Woodward in *Wired*, should be a warning to mavericks (a) to stay off drugs and (b) to stay passive. Rebel actor Belushi was weaned on the anti-Establishment Chicago revue *Second City*. This led to TV satire shows and comments from Belushi that television was crap, the network run by degenerate, mindless pigs. This was telling it to them. But everyone thought Belushi was just terrific. The worse he said, the more they loved him. He made a hit movie, *The Blues Brothers*.

Then the hits became more and more frequently hits of coke: from Captain Preemo's West Hollywood drug menu — Peruvian flake, Bolivian rock, Bubble Gum, *et cetera*. There'd be free-basing binges, binges with twilight girl pushers from Le Hot Tub Club, all-night roaming in limos in search of a line. Most of his $2,000 per diem went on the habit at one time. At least he was spared today's Designer Drugs — synthetic and therefore legal. Also, at times, lethal.

'Success means you can get up and leave when you want to,' said Belushi. Unfortunately, he didn't take his own advice. Desperately trying to get his act

SWORD-SWALLOWER, VENICE BOARDWALK

LA CAGE AUX FOLLES CABARET

together, he took on the movie industry like a speedy Don Quixote tilting at windmills. From Woodward's controversial account, Belushi emerges as a generous, witty and talented man out of control, trapped in a system he both loathes and needs. John Belushi died of an overdose in the Chateau Marmont Hotel on 5 March, 1982. He was thirty-three.

He could have gone far. Instead, he went too far, which used to be Hollywood's unforgivable sin. Sheila Graham, Scott Fitzgerald's cockney gossip-columnist paramour, described how she and Scott lived in separate houses to avoid neighbours reporting her to the Prosecutor of Public Morals. Gossip columnists must be chaste as a Jewish princess. Hedda Hopper saw herself as guardian of morality; Dorothy Parker saw her as Metro-Goldwyn-Merde.

Oral sex was punishable by fifteen years in jail in California. Chaplin was accused of it — with his wife! The evidence was used in the divorce.

Things have naturally loosened up a little since the days when boarding houses had signs up saying 'No dogs, no actors'. In the 1970s, County Strip — an enclave on Santa Monica Boulevard — had educational establishments like The Institute of Oral Love, Climax Prep and Bondage Unlimited. In *Back Home in Tinseltown*, Perelman is also invited to 'Wrestle a Naked Lady — Ten Dollars Back if You Win'.

The only restraint nowadays is the straitjacket when they carry you away screaming. Overdoing everything is doing it just right — décor, clothes, hair, food, drink, drugs. And when I heard recently of someone OD-ing,

THE ROSE BOWL MARKET, PASADENA

SANTA BARBARA

it did not mean over-dosing, but over-dieting, that other great LA indulgence.

Comes the day of reckoning and health food excess, an orgy of *tofu* and low sodium soy sauce. On the wall of our family nutritionist, Doctor An Thanh, the photograph of Carey holds an honoured place below that of President Reagan. Both are good testimonials for this tranquil, humorous Vietnamese who, for reasonable fees, is getting me gradually to resemble that slim, golden youth skipping to Vivaldi. On a diet without dairy products, red meat, salt, sugar, honey, chocolate, cookies, sausages, pasta, alcohol, avocados. What else *is* there?

Modern Donatellos are the cosmetic surgeons, sculpting us to be Beautiful People. Failure in sex and business may result from the slightest deformity, so it is wise to have your acne pits and duelling scars instantly revised by surgery, breasts shaped up by mammaplasty. A bald cosmetic surgeon, who wears a hair-piece for his TV appearance, will give discounts on packages – facelift plus eye-job. Hair transplants are costed by the single 'plug'.

One way or another, we all have to pay for our LA indulgences. Which means finding the doctors' fees, no mean feat if you're a foreigner without Blue Cross. There are exceptions of course. One night, after a

ANIMAL HOSPITAL, MELROSE AVENUE

killing combination of Afghan hash and bourbon, in a state of panicky palpitation I called the Beverly Hills Hotel house doctor. Astonished to find there was not, in this haven for crocks and neurotics, such a person in residence, I had to make do with a phone call. It was a mere 1.30 a.m.

Me Doctor, I think I'm having a heart-attack.
Doc Jesus Christ, you just woke me. . .
Me Sorry about that.
Doc Take a tranquilizer.
Me I don't have any.
Doc Have a hot tub, then.
Me For a heart-attack?
Doc You've got asthma.
Me I never had asthma in my life.
Doc OK, but I'm just warning you – if I come over to the hotel, it's really gonna cost. So here's what you do. Get dressed. Get your car. Drive over here. I'll put a prescription for Librium under the dolphin doorknocker. Don't for Christ's sake ring the bell! Then you go on down to Long Beach where there's an all-night pharmacy. . .

I suddenly felt just fine. It was the best therapy in the world – and cost me nothing but a local call. What a kindly doctor. No wonder the Beverly Hills Hotel recommends him.

Many LA doctors indulge their patients. In his final year, Scott Fitzgerald was prescribed just what he ordered – a diet of coffee, Coca-Cola, lunches of fudge and crab soup, digitalis, benzedrine, and ten Nembutals a night. No wonder it was his last year.

Physical degeneration is one hazard. But no one pays for it worse than the publicly exposed. Fatty Arbuckle, silent movie comedian, was accused of killing a starlet by sexual assault with a champagne bottle. He was acquitted of first degree murder after a hung jury. But it ruined his career. 'How unfair!' commented King Alfonso of Spain, visiting Hollywood at the time. 'It could have happened to any of us.'

Perverted actors, decadent monarchs – 'Moronia' was how H. L. Mencken described LA. But other big literati seem to have been schizoid about it, suffering from a mixture of guilt and glut: guilt about the time they should have been spending writing The Great American (or British) Novel instead of being paired with some hack, wrangling about credits; glut from the booze, beauties and poolside lassitude.

Raymond Chandler, my favourite grouser, was an Anglo-American public schoolboy in revolt, raising the detective story to heights beyond the 'Who-Cares-

JIM BERNSTEIN'S POOL, BENEDICT CANYON

A BEECHWOOD HOME

Who-Killed-Roger Ackroyd?' syndrome, with spirit of place and depth of character rare in the medium. After being fired from a lucrative LA oil job, he was tough on the rich. 'That's the difference between crime and business. For business you gotta have capital.' Philip Marlowe is an educated, chess-playing toughie who could have done better for himself if he were not such a knight in tarnished armour, toting his conscience round the seamier haunts of LA like a rusty lance. Chandler loved the way Humphrey Bogart played him in *The Big Sleep* – for being 'tough

without a gun' and having 'a sense of humour that contains the grating undertone of contempt'.

Chandler enjoyed the clubability of a studio writer's life, but hated the collaborations, finding Billy Wilder just too Germanic and overbearing. He drank heavily to get through his obligations to the studio, which he took seriously. Chandler's creative insecurity and financial security made him typically schizoid: he would joke about Jewish studio executives, then refused to join the La Jolla Tennis Club because, in those days, it would not take Jews. 'My five years in the salt-mines left me a typical case of arrested development,' he admitted. Of screenwriting, he said, 'You go in with the dreams, and come out with The Parent Teachers' Association,' and described the screenwriter as ' . . . the fellow who screams like a stallion in heat and then cuts his wrist on a banana.'

Unlike many writers about Southern California, Chandler spent most of his life there. In a state of love-hate, he turned a sardonic eye on the moral chaos behind those oppulent, Schindler-architected villa façades.

In his world of weak male lushes, ball-breaking flinty ladies and corrupt cops, 'nothing ever looks emptier than an empty swimming pool'. 'Law is where you buy it in this town.' 'This is a big town, Eddie.

THE JOHN MCENROE BUILDING, HOLLYWOOD BOULEVARD

DOWNTOWN LA

Fields. Robert Kennedy was shot live on television by an Arab psycho, while his young son was alone in a hotel room watching it.

The hippie cult hero ('drop out, turn on, tune in') Charles Manson took the hope out of Flower Power by slaughtering, with his acolytes, a group of Bel Air residents including actress Sharon Tate. Joan Didion recalls the rumours: 'There were twenty dead, no, twelve, ten, eighteen. Black masses were imagined, and bad trips blamed. I remember all of the day's misinformation very clearly, and I also remember this, and wish I did not: *I remember that no one was surprised.*' (*The White Album*)

Another revenge by the Superhavenots on the Superhaves was Patricia Hearst's kidnapping by and later allegiance to the Symbionese Liberation Army. Heiress Hearst actually toted a gun for them, and their eventual capture led to the biggest shoot-out in LA police history. Liberals accused the police of brutal attack.

From the *film noir* of the forties (*Farewell My Lovely*) to *Beverly Hills Cop* (1984), LA police get more mocking than pats on the back. They can be quite scary: I was once arrested for walking in Beverly Hills, where they do not like you to use the sidewalk for anything but breakdowns. 'I'm leaving for London in

Some very tough people have moved in here lately. The penalty of growth.' 'The tyres sang on the moist concrete of the boulevard. The world was a wet emptiness.'

Real-life crime, if anything, is even more flamboyant. W. C. Fields said: 'I judge a city's standing, yes, by the quality of its murders. The shoddy, lower-class crimes of late have impinged on the usually high standards of our fair city in the matter of interesting foul deeds ending with a few stiffs. . . '

The sixties would certainly have reassured W. C.

VENICE

CHINATOWN

an hour,' I stammered, afraid of missing my plane. 'An hour's not soon enough, buddy. Get out of town right *now*!'

This is a city where fear is never quite hidden by the fantasy. Fear of the dream becoming a nightmare. Fear of The Night Stalker or The Trashcan Killer. Fear of monthly income not covering the Mercedes payments. Fear the IRS may find you've been cheating on them as well as your wife. Fear your Nicaraguan cleaning lady may buy the house next door. Fear your kids may give up being altar boys and sell secrets to the Russians.

And then quite suddenly the fear is gone, as someone calls to invite you to the Sunday barbecue.

RODEO DRIVE, BEVERLY HILLS

FROSTY MORNING, MALIBU CANYON

COFFEE SHOP AT DUSK, LINCOLN BOULEVARD

DREAMS A REALITY

I stand, immobile as cactus in a Santa Ana wind but a great deal cooler, and wait. Wait for dawn in the desert. It is the hour when normally, just before waking, dreams come vividly to us. But here I am, tinglingly awake, thinking of Harry Dean Stanton's desert lope in Wim Wenders's *Paris-Texas* and the dazzling white Mojave sand in Antonioni's *Zabriskie Point*. What is it about the desert that gets us desertless Europeans?

Silence. Space. The promise of unaccustomed dry heat. And the romance of distant truck lights on Highway 10, bound for Arizona. Still too dark to see the marring jumble of high tension wires. The only high tension comes from Carey, determined her set-up for a tequila sunrise over the San Jacinto mountains will have neither cable nor Marlboro Man billboard in it.

She is blessed, as the technicolor fades in, with an unimpeded view of desert vegetation — 'sage-bush, burro brush and buckwheat, with here and there a strongly gesticulating Joshua-tree, rough barked, or furred with dry prickles, and tufted at the end of its many-elbowed arms with thick clusters of green metallic spikes' (Huxley: *Ape and Essence*). And tall, languid date palms. Date cakes and date shakes are available in Palm Springs, and according to the word of Fodor each date contains a mere twenty-one calories.

We return to our base at Desert Hot Springs. 'Desert

INDIAN CANYON, PALM SPRINGS

what Springs?' exclaimed an LA Grande Dame later. 'Why, that's the Lower East Side of the Desert!'

Ex-band singer with Gene Krupa ('I'm strictly a That Era Person') she bent my ear for much of the eleven-hour flight from Paris with talk of country clubs, celebrities, and her weight problem. At sixty-three, married to a retired businessman, she had realized her dream in the desert: a condo in Rancho Mirage and fifty-eight golf-courses within driving distance (in a golf cart, naturally). But *her* condo had more status than others because it did not actually overlook a golf-course. 'Who wants to see someone else's lousy swing?' she commented, with a That Era delivery worthy of Bette Davis, and sighed to be back at the rancho, losing all those calories gained at European hotels. 'We have a perfect day. Golf in the morning, golf in the afternoon. Dinner at five-thirty. We're in bed by eight.' And she told everything about her life with warmth, humour and intense belief. She really did seem to love every minute of it.

The slogan 'Dreams A Reality' atop a shop in Beverly Hills gave us the theme for this book; sometimes the City of Angels really does deliver a miracle, the desert seem like a promised land.

Palm Springs is The World's Friendliest Place. It has The World's Most Sumptuous Mobile Home Park. It is The Playground of Presidents. It has one pool for every four residents, and aims to reverse those statistics before the year 2000. One of its residents is black, and the Chamber of Commerce fielded any objection by publicly welcoming The Wealthiest Black in America.

Golf is not the name of the game – Making It is. Whatever your race, creed or weight, Making It is the dream. Angelenos are said to be narrow-minded, warm-hearted bores, forever eager-beavering for the fast buck. Some are, but others are open, inventive and enthusiastic.

Success is not necessarily being rich and famous –

THE SPANISH INN, PALM SPRINGS

LAGUNA BASKETBALL GAME

anyone can do that! It is being your own man or woman. A person, free-spirited and individualistic, wearing what you like where you like. It is not just about impressing.

Hence the success of outsiders. Mayor Tom Bradley, hero of the 1984 Olympics razzmatazz, is black. 'A rich man can't buy power, he has to earn his place,' says Bradley. So he once vetoed oil tycoon Armand Hammer's right to drill on Pacific Palisades. Hammer, owing to his influence with the Soviet business community, offered to try and persuade the reluctant Russians to attend the Olympics, on condition he be allowed to drill. The fact that Hammer failed was not held against him, and the veto was waived by the City Council. In Mayor Bradley's view, Hammer had 'earned his place' merely by trying.

Black movie star Eddie Murphy says: 'I won't sell myself down. I will not be packaged and sold like Michael Jackson.' Ironic that the pictures which gave Murphy that choice – *Trading Places* and *Beverly Hills Cop* – are both about blacks making it. Practically the only blacks I've seen in Beverly Hills, by the way, are service employees waiting at the bus stop on Santa Monica Boulevard. So, even in a film, it's good to see Eddie Murphy as Axel, the Detroit cop,

RODEO DRIVE

taking on a WASP Beverly Hills police force, a 'restricted' club, a racially-prejudiced swank hotel clerk – and winning. Comedy comes from the phony liberal front of Axel's antagonists, a wish not to upset until driven to reveal their true colours.

Less grandly than Eddie Murphy, other minority members realize their goals. For Mexican Independence Day, celebrated by the entire Latino population of LA, rival street gangs painted a two-hundred-foot mural in Echo Park, depicting Chicano life in the city. One of the features was the plumed serpent Quetzalcoatl, the Aztec God who symbolizes man's striving for something higher.

President of Channel 34, Spanish language TV, is Danny Villanueva, one of eleven brothers and sisters. Villanueva was born in a two-room earth hut in New Mexico, and now lives in a three-bedroom home in Santa Monica Canyon. A former football champion, he puts in a gruelling seven-day week, burying once and for all the canard about Hispanic sloth: charities, bicoastal business, all-night TV vigils, jogging.

Bettering oneself at every level of society is the basic Angeleno animus.

Gregory Nava's 1984 movie, La Norte, is about Guatemalans trying to better themselves. Along the way, there is much they – and we – find to mock in the mores of prosperity. A Beverly Hills employer ('Call me Gloria, not Señora'), hair freshly coiffed at Jon Peters, shows her perplexed maid, Rosa, how to work a thirty-five-programme washing-machine. In a *shtik* worthy of Chaplin, Rosa fails to tame this domestic monster, and ends up doing the laundry by hand. Gloria returns from tea at Trumps. 'Oh God,' she cries at the sight of sheets drying on the nail-clippered lawn, 'I can't have people *working* around here!'

The Golden North still attracts thousands of immigrants from Central America with dreams of flush toilets and lush kitchens seen in magazines. Many find work before poor American citizens, because illegal labour is cheap labour. By the year 2000 more than half the population of Los Angeles is predicted to be Latino. Making It, to them, is often a case of survival.

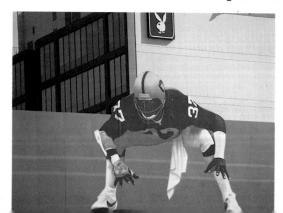

NIKE BILLBOARD

CHINATOWN

approve of women working, because it took work away from the children. And as the actress Dyan Cannon said recently: 'When does anyone make a *Butch Cassidy and The Sundance Kid* with two women?' But there are signs of female muscles flexing — and not just on Muscle Beach.

Joan Didion, Californian novelist and essayist, neatly describes the gulf between the Old and New Woman in *Slouching Towards Bethlehem*. In a 105-degree heatwave, Ms Didion sensibly goes to Ralph's Supermarket in a bikini. A more conventional shopper, in her Hawaiian *muumuu*, does not approve.

' "*What a thing to wear to the market*," she says in a loud but strangled voice. Everyone looks the other way and I study a plastic package of rib lamb chops and she repeats it. She follows me all over the store, to the junior food, to the dairy products, to the Mexican delicacies, jamming my cart wherever she can. Her husband plucks at her sleeve. As I leave the checkout counter she raises her voice one last time: "*What a thing to wear to Ralph's*," she says.'

Not so the Chinese community, who are more established in commerce. Lilly Lee, known as the Asian Queen, is a real estate magnate and one of the few women directors of the Los Angeles Chamber of Commerce.

I had previously thought of LA as a man's town. George Hearst, William Randolph's father, did not

MALIBU BEACH

MAN ON STILTS, PASADENA

A VENICE CLOWN

As though Ralph's were not a supermarket but someone's Bel Air party.

Tackling serious subjects creatively does not seem to daunt LA women. Joan Didion has traced with pungent and agonized pen the violent drift towards self-destruction since the liberating sixties. Martha Coolidge, movie director, made *Real Genius*, about advanced college science secretly used to develop weapons, a timely movie requiring months of research into laser technology.

And Jane Fonda, no less, believes in miracles. Answering a TV interviewer's predictable query as to whether *Agnes of God* resolved issues (they *love* a resolved issue on Channel 2), Fonda said: 'No, but it forces us to question all of those issues. Why am I here? Is there a greater power?' Veering from the left to religion via aerobics, Jane Fonda is my favourite energizer of issues, resolved or not. She exudes enthusiasm, confidence and dedication, whatever the cause.

Another woman, Pat Russell, is a hot candidate for next Mayor of Los Angeles. And the present Mayor of the City of West Hollywood is a lesbian.

Gay Power in LA has long been out of the closet, and evangelical movements like Positive Realism ('Gay To Straight: If you want to make the trip . . . ') are unrealistic in their attempts at conversion. Bravely, many gays are into sexual self-denial, celibacy as a weapon against AIDS; gay actors campaigned on giant billboards against discrimination in the entertainment industry, when screen kissing became a *cause célèbre*. Will AIDS be passed on from one actor to another? Will they suffer the fate of Rock Hudson? It has reached epidemic proportions, with the attendant sense of panic.

But there is a power of spirit among the gay community. And power of spirit is less ephemeral than

HOLLYWOOD PARTY

MUSCLE BEACH, SANTA MONICA

political power. When I visited the late Christopher Isherwood, I was struck by his calm, inner attentiveness. Since encountering the Hindu Monk Swami Prabhavananda here in 1939, Isherwood abandoned the London literary and political scene for a more contemplative life in his peaceful 'dear home' which overlooks Santa Monica Canyon and the Pacific Ocean.

Isherwood describes The Canyon as 'our Western Greenwich Village'.

'It is a shallow, flat-bottomed little valley, crowded with cottages of self-consciously rustic design, where cranky, kindly people live and tolerate each other's mild and often charming eccentricities.' (*Exhumations*)

An ideal place for apostasy: 'After I got to know Prabhavananda, I gradually ceased to be an atheist; because I found myself unable to disbelieve in his belief in God. In due course I became his disciple, a devotee of Ramakrishna and a Vedantist. A liberal I have remained to this day.'

TEMPLES, MALIBU CANYON

Isherwood was always dedicated to a free homosexual society. *Cabaret*, the Broadway musical adaptation of his Berlin stories, shocked him by turning its gay hero into a straight, which he saw as a betrayal. Its film version restored some of the balance by making him AC/DC, but here the offence was Liza Minnelli's far too professional slickness in her interpretation of the rank amateur, Sally Bowles. Although his screenwriting assignments made him well aware of Hollywood's commercial requirements, Isherwood remained a purist where his own original material was concerned.

Another old man whose life might have been entirely devoted to commercial requirements is 100-year-old realtor Henry Lew Zuckerman. Like other members of the largest Jewish community in America outside New York, Zuckerman has, on the contrary, espoused many a charitable cause.

Jewish charities find Israel a long way away these

YOGA TEACHER

days, and often direct their efforts to needs nearer home — retirement homes and schools. They are highly practical, like the Jews who founded Columbia, Universal, Warner, Paramount and MGM; and who still, even in these days of corporate ownership, control much of the LA entertainment business.

Round the corner from the clinic where I had a blood test, I restored myself on Fairfax with the world's best bagels, lox and sour cream. But the new hub of orthodox Jewish life has moved west, to the more fashionable Pico-Robertson area where Steven Spielberg's mother runs a kosher restaurant.

This kind of Jewish homeliness runs through LA's entertainment business. You drop by and pitch a project in a deceptively relaxed, family atmosphere. And the family — Rock, Movies and TV — is very much alive and well in the Leisure Age; most of the world's audio-visual entertainment is produced within a five-mile radius of Hollywood and Vine.

Rock proclaims the power of youth as never before.

Two British schoolday friends of Carey's are now making it as LA video directors. Accusations of porn lyrics and SM images on MTV, the twenty-four-hour video channel, fizzled out with outraged moms, TV Guardians of Morality and Frank Zappa (for the defence) making earnest asses of themselves on chat shows. The Bangles and other girl groups continue to thrive. And though much of the Heavy Metal and Cow Punk may be run-of-the-mill, nothing can drown from memory the wonderful Californian sounds of Fleetwood Mac, the Eagles, Joni Mitchell, Randy ('I Love LA') Newman, and the Doors.

Influences range from far-out contemporary music to Latin American pop and West Coast jazz.

Where else could have a Percussion College with great jazz drummer Shelley Manne for President? The eclecticism about the Hollywood music scene had Stravinsky regularly visiting jazz clubs.

Not another word about Hollywood, I keep telling myself; but, as everyone knows, Hollywood is not a

JONI MITCHELL'S HOME, MALIBU

THE ROSE BOWL MARKET, PASADENA

place but a state of mind, and stays with me like a recurring dream. After all, it does occur in the title of this book. Hollywood, my child, is where deals are made, not dreams. Run largely these days by agents and lawyers and monolithic corporate bodies in New York or San Francisco (anywhere but LA), it makes it on deal-making. A writer friend, typing a letter to a producer who refused to answer his calls, made this Freudian slip: 'Give my love to Marge and the deals.'

Hollywood is also, momentarily, about Scandal Books. No wonder. I even heard the pretty young chief accountant of a block-busting production company tell a colleague: 'But Arnold, I can't just write off a thousand-people party to petty cash. A dinner for twenty at Spago's, okay.' Hence we get the David Begelman Story in *Indecent Exposure* (fraud), Marilyn Monroe and the Kennedys in *Goddess*, The Movie That Ruined United Artists in *The Final Cut*, and The Dolce Vita of Bel Air in *Less Than Zero*. This last horror story has teenage son doing drugs while Mom watches video porn with sisters and movie exec Dad gets a face-lift.

Movie execs have become fashionable as the stars for Scandal Books. It does not upset the old, well-established Hollywood élite; they see these ephemeral characters come and go without much damage to anyone's personal bank balance. Meanwhile the rest of us love to know how lousy life is at the top. In LA, many have already realized their less lofty dreams, and can afford to gloat.

The motion-picture industry, as it's still laboriously called, is rumoured to be moving to less costly climes – Florida, New Orleans, Texas. Perhaps it will then cast less of a shadow over LA's theatre scene. Time and again I hear: 'LA's just not a theatre town.'

Yet, during my last visit, a new theatre opened. Four new theatres, in fact. Bill Bushnell's Los Angeles

UNIVERSAL STUDIOS

'A SMALLER SPLASH'

David Hockney lives and paints here for much of the year, using the Southern Californian light much as Van Gogh and Cézanne used that of Provence. But here the similarity with France ends.

Los Angeles art is traditionally funky. Allen Kaprow began Happenings here way back in the seventies. Edward Kienholz shocked with his Pop Art assemblages. And Edward Ruscha painted the endless linear highways of Los Angeles with no less affection than Van Gogh painted sunflowers.

Portrait artist Don Bachardy showed me his collection of Billy Al Bengston and Ed Moses. 'Trouble is,' he explains, 'there's no art centre. We're all over town, and don't meet that often. An LA artist *must* make it in New York; his potential collectors, even if they live in Beverly Hills, feel safer buying in New York.'

Theater Center on Spring Street is part of a plan to put a shot that is not heroin in the arm of Downtown's Skid Row.

Like the legitimate theatre, LA's art world is overshadowed by the TV and movie industry, which has absorbed so many of its talents. But it has a strong life, very much its own.

With the lively cross-fertilization of graphic and performing arts begun years ago in the heyday of Hollywood, now comes the fusion of art, architecture and technology.

Following the principle of Frank Lloyd Wright in the

CAR MADNESS, WEST HOLLYWOOD

JIM BERNSTEIN'S HOUSE

revolutionary Hollyhock House, built for Alice Barnsdall in 1919, good modern architecture melds with its environment. A big glass window brings nature into the house by day; and by night the lights of LA itself become a sparkling Tiffany window. Surrounded by my indoor plants, I am on a subtly lit 'patio' gazing at Shopping Potential. Outside in, inside out.

Architects since have followed in Lloyd Wright's environmental footsteps. Like the Tewa Indian sculptor, Naranjo, whose luxurious *adobe* desert homes are being built at Chatsworth. This is resort-style living for the bright young technocrat, the man most sought after in LA today.

In technology Los Angeles has a proud record of firsts: 1940 first freeway; 1946 first electronic computer; 1969 first man on the moon.

LA, with its vast aerospace industry, contributed greatly to the realization of that dream. Today it has the greatest concentration of mathematicians, skilled technicians and high technology in the world.

Glenn Curtiss flew the first biplane at Dominguez Field in 1910, and prophesied: 'Los Angeles should be the scene of great developments in the progress of aerial navigation.'

Howard Hughes, founder of TWA and inventor of the world's biggest plane, is described by Joan Didion as 'not merely anti-social, but grandly, brilliantly, surpassingly asocial . . . the last private man'. His gigantic seaplane, Spruce Goose, was reckoned to be about as unflightworthy as The Winged Victory. But it

did make a short lift off the water with Hughes at the controls, surprising the sceptics, before being confined to Long Beach as

HOLLYWOOD BOULEVARD

a rather daunting tourist attraction. Hughes's typically Angeleno perseverance paved the way for Jumbo Jets, although a Boeing 747's wingspan is a paltry 195 feet compared with Spruce Goose's 320 feet.

Hughes Aircraft still comes top of the charts as LA's biggest employer; six aerospace firms are among the top ten. They are, at time of writing, at work on a stealth bomber, a fighter, a spy plane, a patrol craft, and a commercial airliner.

Satellites, spacecraft, strategic, tactical and cruise missiles . . . for all of these, engineers are invited to 'LIVE AND RELAX IN SUN AND SURF'. For artificial intelligence development and state-of-the-art electronics, autonetics and avionics, there are efficient commuter planes to whisk you from Glendale home to Orange County factory with never a whiff of freeway pollution.

Another growth industry is health care. The geriatric boom and lavish third-party insurance reimbursement by companies like Blue Cross have naturally forced up medical costs. It is a sellers' market, with the chairman of a Pasadena-based nursing-home business earning a cool million-and-a-half bucks in one year.

Business-school women graduates are favourites for health care, not doctors. Who needs doctors? It's the creative accountancy that counts.

Then there's the sports medicine business. High-tech rehabilitation is administered to a Yuppy who falls from his polo pony at Griffith Park. At Fitness Diagnostic Centers, biochemical video tells doctors what you are doing wrong at jogging or volleyball. One hundred and fifty kinetic evaluations determine muscle strength around major joints. And, final luxury – transcranial electrotherapy induces deep relaxation. So you can give up meditation, and head for the nearest sports medicine clinic.

Our main worry is: what to do with the leisure. Drugs? Back-pack in the High Sierras? Learn Swahili? Work has been so drummed into us as a virtue, it needs a whole new philosophy to rethink learning as something not necessarily to lucrative ends. In a city with high job potential for the skilled and high unemployment for the unskilled as well, the question is doubly poignant. For all Angelenos, whatever their status in the pecking order. They are a microcosm of the world's social and racial strata – and all exist at different sections of the same long street.

BODY EXPRESS, A HEALTH CLUB

THE ROXY, SUNSET STRIP

Just take a journey east to west down Sunset Boulevard, and you'll see what I mean.

I begin my journey Downtown, where broker meets bum, Yuppy is a block or so from junkie. Past Echo Park, through the anonymous Latino suburb of Silverlake, endless and drab, to Los Feliz. First change of life style. Stop at Chatterton's Bookshop on Vermont, hangout of poet-carpenters and philosophy teachers and other 'endowed loafers' (as William Faulkner called academics); proprietor is anglophile, macrobiotic Koko Iwamoto. Then on to Barnsdall Park, one of the eight Frank Lloyd Wright houses, badly in need of funding and a coat of paint, its grounds overgrown with weeds and winos.

On to the city of West Hollywood, the up-and-coming, not-so-dangerous home of the discerning and well-armed. I love to walk, yes, *walk* up Crescent Heights, cross Hollywood Boulevard where it has become narrow as a country lane, wind my way past the neat homes with tinkling water sprinklers and smell of jasmine, way up to the top; on a crisp, clear winter morning the view is all the way across the city to the ocean and Catalina Island.

Just below, the Boulevard becomes the notorious Strip, where I was once hustled by jailbait in a miniskirt at nine a.m. 'Howya doin', dude?' Nowadays, not

CHATEAU MARMONT HOTEL, SUNSET STRIP

nearly as rough as reputed. Oscar's. respectable English restaurant where two witty retro chanteuses sing 'Chattanooga Choo-Choo'. Past The Diner to Hyatt Hotel, hideaway for rock stars when not at the raunchy Tropicana Motel a block south. At the Roxy they perform; at the Tower, that vast emporium of Pop, I can buy their latest hits, far into the night.

Then everything on Sunset changes, some say for the better. Not I. Granted, the vegetation and lawns and homes of Beverly Hills are beautiful. But too beautiful. It's the emptiness that gets me – like the emptiness of the space where the Arab sheik's house burned down, immolated (they say) for sheer bad taste. Bad taste in Beverly Hills? As though to perish the thought, Sue Ellen's exquisitely garnished granny honks me from her white Mercedes convertible for being slow off a traffic signal. She is in a hurry for Shopping, that sacred rite of Rodeo Drive.

But now I'm at Bel Air, which is all of that, only more so. Calling my name into the microphone hidden in a rock, I am let through the gates of Hugh Hefner's Olde English manor. Two gardeners are discussing an ailing blade of grass. Terrific. The only Redwoods in Southern California. Exotic Japanese fish. Grotto of minah birds, cock-of-the-walks, macaws. Satellite dishes for multi-channel TV. Baby oil in every room. Hair dryers in the pool changing-room ceilings. A bust of Barbie Benton, an organ played by Elton John. Open house Saturday (men over forty dressed in kaftans, girls under thirty in trashy lingerie). But as I meet a retired Playmate, solitary occupant of the rumpus room, with a drink in her hand and a brave smile, it strikes me that the clock stopped some time in the sixties.

Breathe again, as I hit Sunset and continue west, passing the northern end of the University of California, LA. I love the campus, the helpfulness of the research library staff, with their efficient computerized indexing system. Not since my own idle youth at Cambridge have I been to a pleasanter seat of learning; the Hannah Carter Japanese Garden is every bit as beautiful as The Backs. Just right for the contemplative life that may prepare a man or a woman for the work-sharing, sabbatical-taking society of the future.

Now Sunset Boulevard serpents in endless curves to Brentwood, last home of that doomed Angelena, Marilyn Monroe.

RODEO DRIVE SHOPPING PRECINCT

TRASHY LINGERIE, LA CIENEGA BOULEVARD

BACKSTREETS, VENICE

PALM-READER'S HOUSE, VENICE

LIFEGUARD STATION, VENICE BEACH

VENICE

After further leisurely meandering, I reach Pacific Palisades – LA's most evocative T-junction, where Sunset Boulevard ends at the Pacific Coast Highway.

Most people in the Los Angeles area live within twenty miles of the ocean. When it's ninety degrees Downtown, it's seventy-two degrees at the beach. And the changes of beach community north-to-south are as striking as Sunset Boulevard east-to-west.

Why is Malibu still the playground of the stars? Nostalgia, that motive force of so much Angeleno habit? *Nostalgie de boue*, perhaps, as the mud slides come down on you from unstable coastal hills. I've visited some smashing beach homes in The Colony and walked barefoot on sands washed clean by bubbling white water, but it's not till Alice's Restaurant that I really relate to Malibu.

Here, from the pier, I watch surfers on the day of the Equinox, the official end of summer. Over two hundred wait, like immobile birds, to take flight on the big Equinoxal wave. The ocean is calm, too calm. When a rare small wave comes, there is a spirit of comradeship in sharing it. I regret my age suddenly. The nearest I've been to surfing was Frankie Avalon and the Beach Boys.

There have been surf songs, surf movies – now the surf novel. 'The rider sped down the face, drove off the bottom in a powerful turn that sent water spraying in a wide arc from the tail of his board. He drove back up into the face, was nearly covered by a rapidly peeling section. Then he was out of the tunnel, high on the lip, working his board in small rapid turns, racing the wave toward the pier.' (Kem Nunn: *Tapping the Source*)

Continuing south down the coast I hit Santa Monica Pier, my favourite shore area. I, like Christopher Isherwood, have 'a taste for romantic dilapidation'. Muscle Beach, devoted to the body beautiful and wrestling. Chess players and jovial Brits, as though at Brighton, coming down for a pint of Guinness. A minute or two further south by skateboard, the constant carnival of Venice Boardwalk, already eulogized in my preface.

Beach cities, luxurious marinas, quiet canals. . .

On Hermosa Beach, born-again Christians hold outdoor summer services. Status, money and drugs are given up for The Word Of The Lord. Full immersion baptisms no problem.

Palos Verdes, a wooded, hilly peninsular juts out defiantly into the ocean. The Homes Association has made it a closed community, to ensure 'primal verdure'. I drive along the narrow corniche road, taking in Frank Lloyd Wright's glass Wayfarer's

SURFERS, HUNTINGTON CITY BEACH

VENICE BOARDWALK

SANTA MONICA PIER

PALOS VERDES COASTLINE

Chapel. Entry frustrated by a wedding, awkward men suffering tuxedos in the noonday sun, bridesmaids dabbing sweat from their noses.

Lovely for children is the Cabrillo Marine Museum at San Pedro, a kindergarten Sea World. Huge whalebones bear the notice: WHALE GRAVEYARD — PLEASE TOUCH. Again the positive Angeleno approach. Have fun. Enjoy. *Con mucho gusto.*

Nearing Mexico, the sun brighter, the air clearer. . .

Then suddenly I'm at La Jolla, the southern end of the trip. The Costa Geriatrica with sprightly old bodies out for a jog by six-thirty and checking in with the *Wall Street Journal* by eight.

We are wined and dined by Steve Brezzo, young curator of the nearby San Diego Museum of Art. He says casually: 'Thought maybe we'd take you to Mexico for dinner. Just seventeen miles from here to Tijuana.' Steve has that deceptive Californian insouciance covering up a boundless capacity to be doing. Asiatic Art is a speciality of his museum, and he makes several trips a year to the Far East. 'Just hop over to China. Hire a car in Peking and drive around the country. Getting lunch can be a problem.'

Hop over to *China*? My mind is still boggling. But

MARINA DEL REY

LAGUNA BEACH

this, after all, is the Pacific rim. And these are the world's most mobile people.

Even since starting this book Carey and I have moved on. And before finishing, it is time to declare our special commitment. I have become a grandfather in Los Angeles, Carey an aunt. Sasha will be over one year old when the book comes out. What kind of an LA will she grow up in? Joan Didion, during a book promotion tour, kept being asked on TV discussions: 'Where are we headed?' Finally and gratefully, she answered 'Home'.

Sasha's home, despite the prophets of doom, is still rich with possibilities. Hopping over to China. Work-sharing. Sabbaticals. Coming to terms with down-ward mobility. And, who knows, maybe Timothy Leary is not so off-the-wall when he suggests that Los Angeles may eventually secede and become the independent country of Pacifica.

The Far East is the new frontier. There *is* somewhere to move to, after all. We can continue westering to Australia, China, Hong Kong, conquering new markets, buying new art, surfing on new beaches.

Meanwhile, back in Los Angeles or Pacifica, will oranges still grow in the gardens? Will there be big-antlered buck-deer in the Santa Monica Mountains? Ringtail raccoons in Griffith Park? Mountain lions in the canyons? Will I still eat the world's most inventive salads, the best-cooked vegetables? Will azalea and bougainvillaea, acacia and eucalyptus give us shade and sweet scent? Will grunion still hatch their young on the beaches? And humming-birds still sing in the pepper trees?

Perhaps I dreamed they ever did.

JOHN CALAO'S GARDEN, MALIBU

MALIBU

THE VALLEY BY MOONLIGHT

TWO BUNCH PALMS, DESERT HOT SPRINGS

ACKNOWLEDGMENTS

QUOTATIONS FROM BOOKS

F. Scott Fitzgerald 'The Last Tycoon' © Charles Scribner's Sons 1941 Renewal © Frances Scott Fitzgerald Smith 1969. Reprinted by kind permission of Charles Scribner's Sons (US and Canada), The Bodley Head (UK and Commonwealth).

Raymond Chandler 'The Big Sleep' and 'The Little Sister' © College Trustees Ltd. Reprinted by kind permission of College Trustees Ltd and Hamish Hamilton (UK and Commonwealth).

Nathanael West 'Miss Lonelyhearts and The Day of the Locust' Copyright © 1966 by Laura Perelman. Reprinted by kind permission of New Directions Publishing Corporation and Martin Secker & Warburg.

Christopher Isherwood 'Exhumations' Reprinted by kind permission of Curtis Brown on behalf of the Estate of Christopher Isherwood © 1966 Christopher Isherwood; and by kind permission of Candida Donadio and Associates Inc. (USA and Canada).

Aldous Huxley 'Ape and Essence' © Mrs Laura Huxley 1948. Reprinted by kind permission of Mrs Laura Huxley, Chatto & Windus (UK and Commonwealth), Harper & Row (US and Canada).

Joan Didion 'The White Album' Copyright © 1979 by Joan Didion. Reprinted by kind permission of Simon and Schuster (US and Canada) and Weidenfeld & Nicolson (UK and Commonwealth). 'Los Angeles Notebook' from 'Slouching Towards Bethlehem' Copyright © 1967 by Joan Didion. Reprinted by kind permission of Farrar Straus & Giroux (US and Canada) and André Deutsch (UK and Commonwealth).

S. J. Perelman 'Strictly from Hunger', 'Back Home in Tinseltown', 'Genuflections in the Sun' © by S. J. Perelman. Reprinted by kind permission of the Liz Darhansoff Literary Agency on behalf of Abby and Adam Perelman, heirs of S. J. Perelman.

Kem Nunn 'Tapping The Source' © 1984 by Kem Nunn. Reprinted by kind permission of the Dell Publishing Company Ltd.

Budd Schulberg 'What Makes Sammy Run?' © 1941 by Budd Schulberg. Reprinted by kind permission of Schulberg Dorese Agency and Random House.

Evelyn Waugh 'The Loved One' © 1948 by Evelyn Waugh. Reprinted by kind permission of A. D. Peters & Co Ltd and Chapman and Hall Ltd (UK and Commonwealth); and Little, Brown and Company (US and Canada).

W. C. Fields by himself 'His Intended Biography' Commentary by Ronald J. Fields © 1973 by W. C. Fields Productions Inc. Reprinted by kind permission of the publisher, Prentice-Hall, Inc, Englewood Cliffs, New Jersey, USA.

Reyner Banham 'Los Angeles: The Architecture of Four Ecologies' © Reyner Banham 1971. Reprinted by kind permission of Allen Lane The Penguin Press.

QUOTATIONS FROM SONGS

'Hotel California' Written by Don Henley, Don Felder, Glenn Frey. © Cass County Music, Red Cloud Music and Fingers Music. All rights reserved. Used by kind permission of Warner Bros. Music Corporation and Warner Bros. Music Ltd.

'Creeque Alley' by J. Phillips/M. Gilliam. Copyright 1967 MCA Music (a div. of MCA Inc.) New York N.Y. Reproduced by permission of MCA Music Ltd and MCA Music Inc.

Special thanks to friends who appear in the book – Karen (p17), Beverly (p56), Sheila (p59), Camilla and Rachel (p107), Tom Ford (p39), Chad and Carey Hayes (p97), Billy Porter (p113), Amélie Chevalier and Daniel Morgues (make-up and hairdresser for back cover photograph).

And for help with obtaining permissions to quote – Sheila More and Caroline Belgrave.